OUR DIRTY AIR

OUR DIRTY AIR

by SARAH M. ELLIOTT

Illustrated with photographs

Julian Messner   New York

Published by Julian Messner, a Division of Simon & Schuster, Inc.
1 West 39 Street, New York, N.Y. 10018. All rights reserved.

Copyright © 1971 by Sarah M. Elliott

Printed in the United States of America
ISBN 0-671-32467-5 Cloth Trade
ISBN 0-671-32468-3 MCE

Library of Congress Catalog Card No. 70-141833
Design by Marjorie Zaum K.

*To my husband, Paul Elliott; to my editor, Lee Hoffman;
and to Ralph Nader, who inspires us all.*

Contents

1 / Danger in the Air

THE SUMMER OF 1970 began like many others. The days became longer and warmer. The countryside turned greener, and people spent more and more time outdoors. Farmers worked in their fields, homeowners tended their gardens, and city dwellers played and picnicked in the parks.

Then, late in July, something went wrong. On the east coast of the United States, people began to notice that the air was getting dirty. It smelled bad. It looked bad. And every day it got worse. Soon a blanket of dirty air lay over the land from New York all the way to Georgia.

In New York City, people walked the streets with stinging eyes and burning lungs. In Washington, D.C., visitors to the Washington Monument could hardly see the nearby Capitol poking out of the gloom. In Atlanta, Georgia, people drove to work with their car windows tightly closed.

Meanwhile, halfway around the world the skies over Tokyo, Japan, were also getting dirty. At first, the people of Tokyo did not realize how dirty and dangerous the air was becoming. Then the trouble began.

Some high-school girls were playing softball outdoors, as they had many times before. But this time, their eyes began to smart

Gauze masks are better than handkerchiefs as a protection against air pollution. But if these children had clean air to breathe, they wouldn't have to wear anything on their faces.

and they felt sick. When they fell to the ground with coughing attacks, the girls were quickly rushed to hospitals for treatment. The girls recovered. But what had made them so ill? Tokyo's health officials agreed it was the dirty air. They told people to stay indoors as much as possible until the air cleared. But in the next few days, the skies over Tokyo grew dirtier and darker.

Officials went to the beautiful gardens of the Imperial Palace. They inspected all the trees and shrubs and found that many plants were dying. The Emperor and Empress were advised to leave the palace at once. They were told that the clean air of a mountain retreat would be much healthier for the royal family.

Other Japanese families left Tokyo, too. But most of the people could not afford to leave the city; so many of them put on gauze masks to protect them from the dirty air. Some people went out and bought fresh air. A department store began selling oxygen machines for those who could afford them. Other people stopped at small shops around the city for a breath of fresh air. They bought it from small oxygen machines for twenty-five cents a whiff.

In spite of the gauze masks and oxygen machines, many people became ill because of the air. In just one week, over eight thousand people had to be treated in Tokyo's hospitals.

Luckily for the people of Tokyo and the eastern United States, the skies began to clear. Once again, people could safely work and play outdoors. But these were not the only places with bad air in the summer of 1970. People in other parts of Asia and North America complained about bad air. So did people in South America, Europe, and Australia.

For the first time, people everywhere realized that dirty air is now a worldwide problem. As one Japanese scientist put it, unless something is done soon, our skies will turn black and people will have to wear gasmasks all the time.

What is in the air? And how did it become a danger to people in so many different places on earth?

Fresh air in Tokyo sometimes comes from machines. This young woman is enjoying her 25 cents' worth of oxygen in one of the several shops where fresh air is sold.

2 / What Is in the Air

THE AIR AROUND US is a mixture of gases. These gases are invisible, which is why you can't see them. And when the air is clean, you can't smell them either.

One of the gases in the air is oxygen. Every time we breathe, our lungs take oxygen from the air. In our bodies, oxygen combines with food to make the heat and energy we need to live. All living things—people, animals, birds, insects, fish, and plants—need oxygen.

Oxygen is also important to us because it helps to make things burn. Paper, wood, coal, oil, and gasoline would not burn without oxygen. Neither would anything else.

But when fuels such as wood, coal, or gasoline burn, they add other gases to the air. These gases, plus little bits of ash and cinders, dirty the air.

How People Began Dirtying the Air

Millions of years ago, people didn't think much about whether the air was clean or dirty. Except for a forest fire here or a volcanic eruption there, all the air was clean.

Then men learned how to make fires and started dirtying the

When people first invented fire, they also invented air pollution.

air. But there were so few people on earth that the fires didn't dirty the air very much.

Thousands of years went by. Men built towns and cities. They made fires to heat their homes and cook their food. As the cities grew larger, city air became smokier. But the air over most of the earth was still clean.

Then in the nineteenth century, the world and its air began to change rapidly. Farmlands and fields were covered with factories, and thousands of people came to work in them. And thousands of factory chimneys belched soot and smoke into the air.

In the twentieth century, cities grew larger. More and more

factories were built. More people came to work in the cities. Each year, more and more cars and trucks filled the city streets and highways.

The fumes from all the cars and the smoke from all the factories and incinerators (garbage disposal plants) darkened city skies. More and more days were gray and overcast. People began to talk about *pollution*. They found that many things dirtied or *polluted* the air. Each of these things is called a *pollutant*. Most of the pollutants we know about are gases. Some pollutants such as soot and cinders are called *particles*.

How Cars Pollute Our Air

A few years ago, people going to a rock concert in Boston parked their cars in an underground garage. After the concert, they all got into their cars and tried to leave. There was a delay because each driver had to pay a parking fee as he left. As cars waited with their engines running, the garage began to fill with fumes.

People started to feel sick and dizzy. Soon, they were running and staggering out of the garage. They fell to the ground coughing and choking. Other people fainted in their cars and had to be carried into the open air.

One garage official realized what was happening. He quickly ordered the fee takers to let all the cars drive out without paying. If he had not acted so quickly, some of the people could have died of the fumes.

When the garage was cleared, twenty-five people had to be rushed to the hospital. Many others were treated and sent home.

The pollutant that caused all the trouble is a colorless, odorless gas called *carbon monoxide*. Small amounts of carbon monoxide can give you a headache or make you sick to your stomach. Large amounts of this poison can make you drowsy, dopey, and cause death.

Car exhaust fumes also contain *hydrocarbons*. These pollutants don't work as fast as carbon monoxide but they are poisons just the same. Hydrocarbons come in all shapes and sizes. Almost two hundred different kinds of hydrocarbons fly out of car exhausts. Others come from burning coal, boiling tar, burning leaves, and the smoke stacks of incinerators.

Car exhaust fumes fill the air with particles as well as gases. Some of the most dangerous ones are *lead* particles. In recent years, lead has been added to gasoline to make car engines run more smoothly. But lead in the gasoline means lead particles come out of the tailpipe. Now, some of the oil companies are working to take the lead out of their gasoline. But there is still too much of this pollutant in the air.

These are only some of the pollutants that come from cars. There are many more. They fill the air where traffic is heavy. Car fumes are harmful to everyone, but especially to the people who have to drive or work in heavy traffic.

Recently, there was an unusual strike in New York City. It involved a labor union, which has members who collect tolls in the tunnels and on the bridges around the city. The toll collectors were not asking for more money. They wanted clean air!

Anthony Mauro, the head of this union, explains why: "Thousands of cars go back and forth every day. Each car stops to pay a toll. When the car starts up again, it leaves behind a cloud of fumes. So my men are being made to work in air that is thick with pollution." No wonder the toll collectors went on strike for cleaner air!

How Factories Pollute the Air

The trouble with most factories is that what goes up their chimneys comes down on us. Smoke and soot, ash and cinders come puffing out of factory chimneys to speckle our clothes and get into our lungs. And the smoke from factories and power plants contains many different pollutants.

Some of these pollutants are a family of gases called *sulfur oxides*. (Sulfur dioxide is the most common member of this family.) Sulfur oxides can shorten the life of whatever they touch. They wear away paint and eat into the surface of statues and stone buildings. They damage crops and are harmful to people.

Another family of gases that come from smokestacks are *nitrogen oxides*. These gases color the air a dirty yellow-brown and give it a bad smell. Nitrogen oxides come from factories that make explosives and fertilizers. They also come from burning leaves (as do hydrocarbons). That is why more and more cities and towns tell people not to burn their leaves.

A city full of factories and power plants is a city full of dirty air.

Dirty air means dirty statues in Washington, D.C. This stone statue of a famous American named Alexander Hamilton was once clean and bright. Now look at it!

Many people think that a tiny amount of *fluoride* in toothpaste and drinking water is good for your teeth. But did you know that fluoride is also a dangerous pollutant?

Fluoride gas and particles pollute the air around factories that make chemical fertilizers. Aluminum plants, oil refineries, copper smelters, and glass brick factories also dirty the air with fluoride gas and particles.

Factory fluorides can harm plants, animals, and people. Fluorides have eaten paint off buildings and rotted fences in Florida. They have ruined crops of tomatoes, peppers, peaches, and cherries in Washington and Oregon. They have killed pine trees in Washington. They have crippled and killed cattle in Florida and Montana.

Asbestos is a very useful mineral because it does not burn. It can be mixed with plastic, cement, cloth, and many other things to make them fireproof. That is why asbestos is put in plaster, paint, linoleum, roofing, siding, ironing-board covers, pot holders, movie screens, and automobile brake linings.

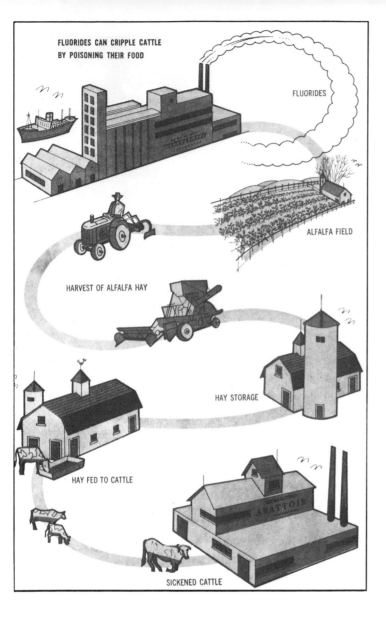

FLUORIDES CAN CRIPPLE CATTLE
BY POISONING THEIR FOOD

FLUORIDES

ALFALFA FIELD

HARVEST OF ALFALFA HAY

HAY STORAGE

HAY FED TO CATTLE

SICKENED CATTLE

This was once a healthy cow. Now it is crippled by a bone disease caused by fluoride poisoning. Soon it will die.

But when these things are made in factories, *asbestos dust* gets into the air. This is dangerous because factory workers who breathe in asbestos particles can get lung diseases. In the past, only the people who worked in asbestos mines or asbestos factories were harmed. But today, asbestos is used in so many ways that it is a danger to all of us.

For example, asbestos dust pollutes the air when construction workers use it to fireproof a building. It gets into the air when car brake linings wear out. And it gets into the air when pot holders and other household items wear out and asbestos particles are released.

Materials other than asbestos can resist fire and may be safer to use. Scientists are experimenting to find a way to make more things fireproof and *safe*.

Pollution and Sunshine

So far, you have been reading about pollution that comes from cars and factories. There is another kind, called *photochemical* air pollution.

Here is how photochemical pollution is made. On a warm day when the sun is shining, factories and cars fill the air with particles and gases. These pollutants react to the sunlight. They regroup and form new chemical combinations. These new combinations form an ugly poisonous haze over the city. The people of Los Angeles call it smog.

Photochemical smog has been a problem to Los Angeles for years. Now the problem goes beyond city limits. Polluted air drifts over the surrounding countryside to poison small plants

Los Angeles has lots of sunshine and more cars than any other city. The sunlight and car fumes combine to give the city lots of something else —smog.

and large trees. This is why some fruits and vegetables can no longer be grown near Los Angeles and other smoggy cities.

Pesticides and Other Chemical Sprays

Have you ever seen an exterminator at work? He sprays floors and walls with special chemical poisons to kill flies, ants, cockroaches, termites, and other pests. The chemicals he uses are called *pesticides*. Large amounts of pesticides are also used outdoors to kill insects that eat crops, damage trees, or carry disease.

Some poisonous sprays are used to kill weeds and unwanted plants. These plant killers are called *herbicides*.

An airplane sprays chemicals over farmlands in the Middle West. Half of these chemicals may be carried by the wind to other places.

People use airplanes to spray large tracts of land with chemicals. The pilot swoops low over the land, spraying as he goes. Some of the spray lands on the ground. But some of it is blown away in the wind and floats to places where the poison is not wanted. When villages and parks are accidentally sprayed, the poisons can kill songbirds and small animals.

Pesticides and herbicides are harmful to people, too. They can poison food, crops, and water. They have even made farm workers very sick. Some of the workers drank water near land that was sprayed. Others were accidentally sprayed while they were working in the fields. Still others were told to go back into the fields too soon after spraying. Some fields are still not safe a month after they have been sprayed.

Citizens' groups are now urging the Department of Agriculture to stop all use of such chemical sprays as DDT, heptachlor, lin-

Curtis Boyette and his father live on a tobacco farm in North Carolina. One night, Curtis's seven-year-old brother mysteriously died in his sleep after working in the tobacco fields. A short while later, Curtis became sick and had to be rushed to the hospital. Doctors later discovered that both boys had been poisoned by parathion. Parathion is a very strong insecticide which is used to kill tobacco worms and other pests. Like many other farmers, Mr. Boyette has stopped using parathion.

dane, aldrin, endrin, dieldrin, and chlordane. They also want to get rid of herbicides such as 2, 4, 5-T. All of these chemical sprays are deadly, and their use and effects cannot be controlled. So far, the Department of Agriculture has limited the use of some of these poisons, but none of them has been completely banned.

3 / Air Pollution and the Weather

How Nature Cleans City Air

People decide how much pollution is put into the air over their cities. But nature decides what happens after that. If the city is lucky, some of the pollution is carried away by the wind.

Some cities are more windy than others. New York and Chicago are among them. Fresh winds from the Atlantic Ocean help clean out New York City's air. Southwest winds blow Chicago's dirty air out over Lake Michigan.

Unlucky Los Angeles is not a windy city. Pollution collects over the city faster than it can be blown away. But even Los Angeles is windy some of the time.

Airplane pilots say that on a really windy day they can see a long plume of smog blowing from Los Angeles out across the Pacific Ocean. When the wind blows the other way, Los Angeles smog blows all the way to Denver, Colorado!

Even when a city is not windy, nature has ways to air it out. The sun heats city streets and buildings which, in turn, heat up the air around them. Soon the city air is hot enough and light enough to rise. Up it goes to mix with clean air high above the city. Eventually, high-flying winds blow the dirty air away.

Nature's winds and rising-hot-air system work pretty well for

Dirty air sometimes hides Chicago's skyscrapers. Years ago, people in the city used to complain about how windy it was. But nowadays, some Chicagoans wish that the Windy City was even windier, so that the winds would get rid of the air pollution when it hangs over the city.

small loads of pollution. But winds and rising air cannot clean the air of the largest and dirtiest cities quickly enough. In these places, there is always some pollution in the air.

Air Pollution and Bad Weather

Sometimes the weather makes city air much worse. This happens when hot air does not rise. If the air doesn't rise, the pollution won't either.

Most days, warm city air rises to the cool air high above. But sometimes, a large mass of warm air moves over the city and stays there. The warm air mass traps city air underneath it.

This is downtown Los Angeles during an inversion, when a "lid" of warm air prevents the polluted air from rising. The air is much clearer above the lid. On a day like this, it is much better to have an office near the top of City Hall (the tall building in the middle) than down near the ground.

When this happens, weathermen call it an *inversion*. They mean that the layers of hot and cold air have been reversed, or inverted.

During an inversion, city air rises to meet the lid of warm upper air. Fog and polluted air from the city are trapped under the lid. After several days, thick smog covers the city. Unless a strong wind or heavy rain comes along, the city air will get worse. And dirty polluted air will be a health hazard to all the people who live there.

In the past, the worst inversions happened in winter. But beginning in 1970, pollution experts began to worry about inversions happening all year round.

27 / *Air Pollution and the Weather*

4 / How Air Pollution
Harms Living Things

Pollution and Plants

About twenty years ago, people began to notice something was wrong with certain forests in southern California. They saw that many ponderosa pines turned yellow, dropped their leaves, and died. No known insects or diseases could be blamed for what was happening to the trees.

Then they discovered that photochemical smog was poisoning the trees. But where could the smog be coming from? There are no highways and factories deep in the forests. Eventually, weather experts found that winds carried the smog all the way from Los Angeles, some eighty miles away.

Today, millions of trees are dead or dying from pollution. And these weakened trees are easy victims for insects. Tree experts are trying to grow new trees that can resist smog. But in the meantime, beautiful forests are being destroyed—not only in California but also in the eastern part of the United States and in Canada.

Other plants are suffering, too. Various kinds of air pollution have damaged citrus fruits, grapes, peaches, tobacco, lettuce, spinach, and other crops all over the country.

Because the effects of pollution show up much more quickly in plants than in animals or people, experts use plants to study

There was a time when these two Ponderosa pines looked alike. Now the one on the left is dying because of the smog in the San Bernardino Mountains. The tree on the right is lucky to survive, but it too may die—unless the air is cleaned up.

A U.S. Department of Agriculture plant expert compares two potato plants. You don't have to be an expert to tell which plant was grown in polluted air and which in clean air.

the effects of different pollutants. They have learned that tulips and corn are poisoned by fluorides but not by sulfur dioxide. Alfalfa, dandelions, and cotton are damaged by sulfur dioxide but not by fluorides. The experts also found out something else: no plants can resist *all* kinds of pollution.

Pollution and Animals

What does pollution do to animals? We know that strong pesticides can kill songbirds, and fluorides can cripple and kill cattle. What about other animals?

Many zoo animals have been affected by air pollution. These animals are easier to study than ones in the wild because they stay in one place and get regular medical checkups.

In the Philadelphia Zoo, a large number of animals have developed lung diseases in recent years. Some of them have even died of lung cancer. In the Chicago Zoo, some of the polar bears have lung diseases, too. And at the Ueno Zoo in Tokyo, the polar bears have turned from white to sooty gray. In that same zoo are monkeys that have developed thick clumps of hairlike skin inside their noses to filter out the dirty air.

These are just a few scattered reports. We need to know much more. What does air pollution do to the chickens, sheep, hogs, and other animals that provide us with food? What does pollution do to pets? Right now doctors, scientists, and government experts are beginning to find some answers to these questions.

Pollution and People

Dorothy is a little girl who lives in Chicago. Some days her mouth bleeds and her gums are so swollen she cannot eat. From time to time she runs a fever and has pains in her fingers and knees. At other times she has a bad stomachache or is too tired to play.

Dorothy's older brothers and sisters get skin rashes and dizzy spells. Some days, when the air stinks of pollution, the whole family feel sick to their stomachs.

Dorothy had had many hospital tests, but the doctors can find no disease. However, one of her doctors says she is sick from polluted air. There is good reason to think he is right. When Dorothy gets away from the factories and superhighway in her neighborhood, she begins to feel much better.

Children in other places have suffered from air pollution, too. In Los Angeles and Tokyo, children have felt sick and keeled over on smoggy days. Now if they are at school in dirty weather,

Sometimes people, animals and birds all speak the same language.

the children are kept indoors during recess. And they are told not to run, skip, or hop on their way home.

These children in Los Angeles and Tokyo are good examples of how air pollution affects *healthy* people. Dirty air has worse effects on people who are already ill.

"I just don't seem to be able to get rid of this cough." "I've had this cold of mine for weeks." You have probably heard many people say these things. Doctors believe that air pollution can make a cough or cold worse. In other words, pollution can stop people from getting well quickly.

Asthma, bronchitis, and emphysema are all serious diseases of the lungs. If people have these diseases and breath polluted air, their lungs will get worse and worse.

Today, more and more people are suffering from lung diseases. In fact, emphysema is the fastest-growing cause of death in the United States. We also know that air pollution is getting worse each year. Does this mean that air pollution can cause lung diseases? Some doctors and scientists now think so.

"What's the matter? Got something in your eye?" Air pollution makes eyes and throats burn.

Probably the most feared lung disease is *lung cancer*. Scientists still don't know all the things that can cause it. They already know that asbestos dust can lead to cancer. So can certain hydrocarbons in cigarette smoke. That is why there is a message printed on every pack of cigarettes that says, "Warning: The Surgeon General Has Determined That Cigarette Smoking Is Dangerous to Your Health."

Scientists have discovered that the *same* hydrocarbons found in cigarette smoke are also found in polluted air. They say that breathing dirty air may be just as harmful as smoking cigarettes. So the people who breathe dirty air and who smoke, too, are taking a great risk. They may be the future victims of lung cancer.

Disaster!

Sometimes the air becomes so polluted that many people in a city may become very sick and some may even die. When this happens, we call it a *disaster*.

The first big air-pollution disaster happened over forty years ago in Belgium. Factories, coke ovens, blast furnaces, and steel mills in the Meuse Valley filled the air with soot and smoke. Then a thick blanket of fog covered the valley for several days. The air became dark and dangerous. Before it cleared, thousands of the people were sick and sixty of them died.

The first United States disaster happened in Donora, Pennsylvania. Donora is an industrial town surrounded on all sides by high hills. In October, 1948, fog covered the city for a week. An inversion kept the city air down and the hills kept it in. The

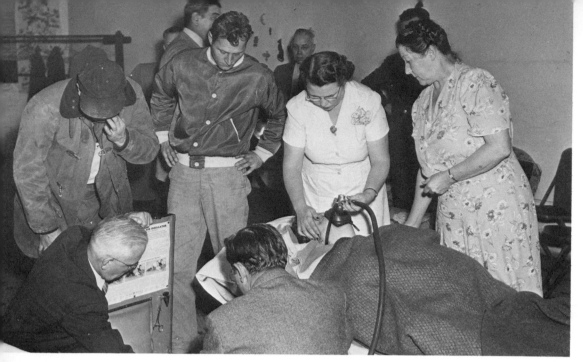

A nurse gives oxygen to an air-pollution victim in Donora, Pennsylvania, during the first U.S. air-pollution disaster. Since then, thousands of other Americans have had to have the same kind of treatment.

Donora in 1949, one year after the air-pollution disaster. Factories continued to dirty the town's air.

trapped air became dirtier and dirtier. Nearly six thousand people got sick and twenty people died.

In the 1950's and 1960's, New York City had four large air-pollution disasters which took the lives of over eight hundred people. Other American cities have also suffered disasters in recent years. For example, in 1969, Chicago had three periods of dirty air that took the lives of one hundred people.

The world's worst air-pollution disaster happened in London, England. In December, 1952, thick fog covered the city and blotted out the sun. Airports shut down and traffic stopped. But the chimneys of London kept puffing away.

The smoggy air was still, cold, and poisonous. It made people's eyes and throats burn. Soon the hospitals began filling up.

After four days, the skies cleared. By that time, four thousand people were dead and many others were ill. In the next two months, eight thousand more people died from the pollution poisoning in that disaster.

Most newspapers don't talk about air-pollution disasters anymore. Instead they copy the doctors and pollution experts who prefer to talk about *episodes*. By episode they mean a period of time when the air is badly polluted and when more people than usual go to the hospital for treatment. We could say that episodes are just not-so-bad disasters. But whatever we call them, they are dangerous.

5 / What Can be Done About Air Pollution

RIGHT NOW, dirty air from the cities is spreading farther and farther into the countryside. Air pollution episodes happen more and more often. And the air is getting dirtier between episodes.

Each year, more and more cars are manufactured and factories built. And since cars and factories produce most of the pollution, the air is getting worse.

Cars produce over half of all the pollution in this country. So to clean up the air, we must first clean up the cars.

Cleaner Cars

Some American cars are fitted with pollution-control equipment. The controls keep certain pollutants from leaving the engine and pouring out the tailpipe. Since 1968, every new car sold in the United States must have some pollution controls. This is a national law. But most Americans drive older cars that don't have pollution equipment. So most of the cars on the roads continue to dirty the air.

Although new cars pollute less than old ones, they are far from perfect. The pollution controls won't work well unless the car's engine is kept in very good condition. Even then, the control system stops only some of the pollutants from getting into the air.

The cities of Louisville, Kentucky (above) and St. Louis, Missouri (below) have one problem in common: air pollution.

There are some pollutants for which we have no controls at all. Lead in gasoline is one of them. It goes right through the pollution-control equipment and out into the air. Some lead particles remain inside the car. In time, they clog the control system and keep it from working well. Some gas stations now sell unleaded gasoline.

More and more people believe that to clean up the air we must stop using gasoline—either leaded or unleaded. If so, what other fuels could be used?

Some auto engineers have been experimenting with car engines that burn natural gas. They find that natural gas gives off much less pollution than gasoline does.

Other engineers have been designing new car engines. Some of these cars run on electric batteries. Others run on steam. *Electric cars* make no pollution and *steam cars* make only a little. *Hybrid cars* are designed to have two engines. They run on electricity in the city and gasoline in the country. All of these cars would cut down city pollution.

New clean cars may be on the market soon. But it will be years before all the old gasoline-engine cars are off the highways. So what else can be done?

Many people believe the way to clean up city air is to get rid of *all* cars. Think what this would mean to Los Angeles, where over 80 percent of the dirty air comes from cars!

But the people of Los Angeles need their cars to get to work. The city has few buses and no subways or local trains. The same is true of many other cities. Chicago, Philadelphia, and New York have many buses, subways, and trains—but not enough to handle

This is an experimental electric car made by General Motors. It is small, quiet, and easy to drive. Most important of all, it does not pollute the air. It is only one of the many different electric cars now being tried in the United States and other countries.

Take a look "inside" the GM electric car. A small electric motor (Coaxial DC Motor) drives the rear wheels of the car. Electricity from the batteries under the floor turns the motor.

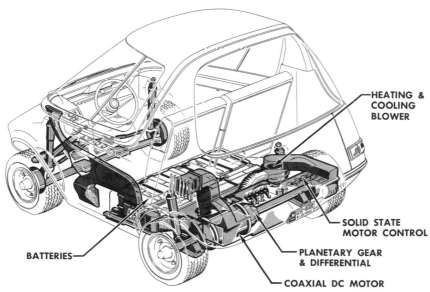

HEATING &
COOLING
BLOWER

SOLID STATE
MOTOR CONTROL

BATTERIES

PLANETARY GEAR
& DIFFERENTIAL

COAXIAL DC MOTOR

This enormous chimney is as high as the Empire State building. It is in Copper Cliff, an industrial town in Ontario, Canada. It was built to make sure that sulfur dioxide and other pollutants from the factory below would rise higher, spread thinner, and blow farther away.

all the people. So until more public transportation is built, the people cannot give up their cars.

Cleaner Smokestacks

To clean up their pollution, some factories and power plants have built very high smokestacks. Pollutants go up and out the stacks and winds carry them away. This cleans up the air for people who live and work nearby. But the pollution from the factories may land on people who live hundreds of miles away.

High smokestacks have helped to clean the air in England. But the pollution from these stacks blows miles across the sea and is dumped on Norway and Sweden! So high stacks just spread the dirt farther.

Some factories in this country use huge machines to clean their smoke before it leaves the stack. These machines can remove all large particles from the smoke. But small particles leave the stack, float in the air, and get into your lungs. One of these machines can also remove some sulfur dioxide—the worst factory pollutant.

Not enough factories and power plants use these machines. And there are no machines that can remove all the gases and particles from factory smoke. Therefore, we need better pollution controls for factory smoke.

Cleaner Industrial Fuels

Many factories in the country use coal and oil that are low in cost but rich in sulfur. Most of the power plants which make electricity burn cheap coal. When these fuels burn, they fill the

When a major steel company built a new steel mill at Burns Harbor, Indiana, they included some air-pollution control equipment. Enormous "wet scrubbers" (which look like huge metal barrels) can remove particles and some sulfur oxides from the smoke before the smoke goes up the chimney.

air with sulfur dioxide and other pollutants. So the power plants are the biggest source of industrial pollution in the United States.

Oil can easily be desulfurized before it is burned. Coal cannot be desulfurized. We have large supplies of coal that have almost no sulfur, but the coal companies must dig new mines to get to these supplies. If more industrial plants used clean oil and clean coal, we would have much less pollution.

One of the cleanest industrial fuels is natural gas. Natural gas doesn't contain sulfur so it doesn't give off sulfur dioxide when

This is what the wet particles look like after they leave the wet scrubber. Without this wet scrubber, the blast furnace would have thrown all of that dirt into the air!

it burns. It doesn't give off particles, either. Many factories and power plants could and would use natural gas if it weren't so expensive.

There is one *very* cheap fuel that power plants can use to make electricity. It is garbage. When garbage is burned in special furnaces instead of open dumps, its pollutants can be controlled. Every city makes plenty of garbage daily.

Some European cities have been burning garbage to make electricity since World War II. They began doing it because they had no other fuel. Since the United States makes more garbage than any other country, it is time we try this system, too.

Some power plants don't pollute the air because they don't burn *any* fuel. These are *hydroelectric* plants. In these plants, the power of falling water is changed into electricity. There are many hydroelectric power plants near rivers and dams in the United States.

Another kind of clean power plant uses hot water and steam from deep in the ground. Pipes are dug into the ground and hot water and steam rise to the surface. The hot water cools in ditches and the steam is piped into the plant to make electricity. Steam power plants are already used in Mexico, Iceland, Italy, and New Zealand. Scientists say these plants could be built in many parts of the western United States where we have huge underground beds of steam and hot water.

6 / What Government Should Do About Air Pollution

EVERYONE IN THE UNITED STATES has the right to breathe clean air. But who or what is responsible for making sure we actually do have clean air? It is the government—city, county, state, national, and international.

A Tale of Two Cities

Years ago, the people of Pittsburgh decided to do something about their city. Smoke from the steel mills and from coal-burning train engines blackened the skies. Often it was so dark that city lights had to be turned on in the middle of the day.

In 1945, Pittsburgh set up smoke-control programs. In time, the skies cleared over the city because the programs were carried out.

The people of Los Angeles also decided to improve their air. In 1947, they passed laws to clean up factories, power plants, garbage dumps, and junkyards. Soon the skies over Los Angeles began to clear.

The people of Pittsburgh and Los Angeles passed laws and saw that they were carried out. That is why the air in these two places became cleaner.

Pittsburgh before its air was cleaned up: the air is thick with pollution. Trucks, cars, and stores have their lights on, even though it's not even nine o'clock in the morning!

This is the same street in Pittsburgh a few years after the city started its successful smoke-control program.

How Government Has Helped Clean Up Cars

Although the air over Los Angeles became cleaner, it was not clean enough. What else could be causing pollution? In 1950, Professor Arlie Haagen-Smit proved that the pollutants coming out of car tailpipes were causing photochemical smog. Officials of Los Angeles asked the auto companies to make cleaner cars. For many years, nothing happened.

Finally, the Los Angeles officials got the California legislature to pass a law saying that only cars with pollution controls could be sold in their state. The auto companies began to worry because they were selling more cars in California than in any other state. They decided to put in controls.

In 1968, the United States government followed California's lead. Congress passed a law requiring pollution controls on every new car in the country.

Now California laws call for even cleaner cars by 1975. They will test all new cars for a number of different pollutants. Only tiny amounts of pollution will be allowed.

Auto officials say they cannot follow these laws. They need more time. But that is what they said the last time. However, California officials are determined to have clean cars on the highways. Because they do not believe gasoline-engine cars can be made clean enough to meet the standards of their laws, they are

This is the city of Los Angeles on one of those rare days when the air is clear. The people who live there want the air to be this clean *every* day. That is why California passed laws against cars that pollute the air.

now testing cars with new engine designs. California is telling the big auto companies they will have to make *clean* cars or keep their cars out of the state.

In 1970, the federal government passed a clean air law that will cut car fumes by 90 percent. This law will limit hydrocarbons, carbon monoxide, and nitrogen oxides by 1976.

From the city of Los Angeles to the state of California to the rest of the United States—this is an example of how people can work through their governments to get cleaner cars.

Government and Smokestacks

Almost every city and state in our country has air-pollution laws for factories and power plants. Some of these laws are good ones, but each law affects only a small part of the country. And in many places, the laws have not been carried out.

These men are using a special machine to measure all of the gases coming out of a nearby smokestack. Each gas has a different pattern of invisible rays that the machine can "see." Such machines tell how much of each gas is coming out of the smokestack.

What happens if a city or state cleans up its factories, and then winds bring in pollution from a neighboring state? What if smokestack dirt from New Jersey drifts over to New York? Who can settle the problem?

Only the federal government can control smokestack pollution. If federal laws are carried out, it will mean cleaner air for the people in every state.

In 1970, the federal government made new laws for clean air. These laws will limit the major pollutants from smokestacks (as well as cars). Smokestacks in all the states will have to be cleaned up in the 1970's. And each state government will have to make sure that the federal laws are obeyed.

Because of the 1970 laws, private citizens can now take polluters to court. If the citizens win the case, the polluters can be forced to clean up or close down. Citizens can also take government agencies to court if they don't act against polluters.

Over the years, many people in different federal departments have handled the control of our environment—air, water, waste, radiation, and pesticides. Then President Richard Nixon decided to take all these scattered departments and put them under one roof. In December of 1970, he started a new agency called the Environmental Protection Agency (E.P.A.). One job of this new agency is to see that the clean air laws are carried out.

The Environmental Protection Agency decided not to wait many years to limit some pollutants. In 1971 they set standards for sulfur oxides, particles, carbon monoxide, nitrogen oxides, and hydrocarbons.

Air pollution does not stop at the boundaries of countries any

The official symbol for the United Nations Conference on the Human Environment, Stockholm, June 5 to 16, 1972.

more than it does at state lines. For example, the people of Windsor, Canada, get dirty air from the factories of Detroit, Michigan. And Norway gets pollution from Germany.

More and more people believe we need *world* laws against air pollution. So someday soon, you may read about the United Nations passing these kinds of international laws.

Needed—More Clean Fuel

The United States government can also help us in the fight against air pollution by making sure we have enough clean fuels for factories and power plants.

Some of the major fuel companies that sell natural gas, oil, and coal say that they don't have enough supplies of clean fuel. Is that really true?

The natural gas companies keep the records of their supplies a secret. So nobody knows how much natural gas we actually have in this country. Pollution experts now say the federal government should make a study of these supplies as soon as possible.

They say that if there are large supplies, the gas companies should be forced to sell more gas at a lower price. This would mean that more factories, power plants, and cars could use this clean fuel.

As for oil, according to federal law there is a limit on the amount that can be imported into the United States from foreign countries. This limit helps the U.S. oil companies to keep their prices up, but they claim they have a shortage of clean oil. Pollution experts have advised the government to change the laws and allow more foreign oil to come in. Then the U.S. companies could desulfurize it, and we would have more clean oil—and it would be cheaper.

These two "sniffers" on a rooftop high above the streets of Pittsburgh are used to measure air pollution. They take in polluted air and send information about it to a special computer every five minutes. In this way, the local government knows about the city's air any time of the day or night.

The coal companies also claim there is a shortage of clean coal. But according to government studies, we have plenty of clean coal that has not been mined. Of course, the coal companies don't want to spend the money to open expensive new mines. Instead, they want to continue selling their huge piles of cheap, high-sulfur coal. So the government may have to force the coal companies to give us clean coal.

Federal, state, and city governments can force polluters to clean up the air. But first of all, the people must make these government officials realize how important it is that they do their job. This is why air-pollution control is really up to the people.

7 / What You Can Do About Air Pollution

UNLESS YOU, YOUR FAMILY, your neighbors, and friends take an interest in stopping air pollution, nothing will be done about it. You can start by forming a Clean Air Club. Ask your friends and classmates to join the club. If you are a scout, you can talk to your scoutmaster about forming a club. Perhaps the entire troop will want to be members.

The first thing your club should do is find out about the air-pollution laws in your community. This means finding out about city, state, and federal laws.

You can arrange for your Clean Air Club to pay a visit to the mayor of your community. Ask him about clean air laws and how they are being carried out. What is being done about dirty factories and power plants? Are people allowed to burn leaves and trash? And what happens to people who break the clean air laws?

Your club should also find out about cars. Visit the local office of the state department of motor vehicles. Ask the officials there to explain pollution-control equipment and how it works. Ask them to tell you the laws about cars that give off too much pollution.

Even new cars with pollution controls won't work well unless

In this neighborhood, both children and adults need to do something about the air in which they work and play.

they have a tune-up. Ask your teacher to invite an auto mechanic to visit your class. Get him to explain how frequent tune-ups keep cars clean. Then find out how many of your classmates' family cars have had tune-ups lately. Check each month and keep a record of the results.

Ask your parents if the family car can pass this test:

1. The *engine, carburetor,* and *ignition* are in good working order.
2. The *spark plugs* are clean.
3. The *pollution-control system* works well.
4. The car burns *lead-free gasoline.*

Your Clean Air Club can also find out about air pollution by writing letters. You can write to your U.S. representatives and senators. You should also write to your State Pollution Control Board or to one of the ten regional offices of the Environmental Protection Agency. Your local librarian will be able to help you find the right addresses.

The members of your club can do more than ask people about air pollution. They can become air-pollution detectives. This kind of detective work is something you can do by yourself. All you need is one pad, one pen, and two sharp eyes.

Try to make air checks of factories, power plants, city dumps, apartment houses, backyard incinerators, and any other places that may pollute the air. Do this regularly—once a week or several times a month.

Look for smoke and soot. If you see some, write down what you

Some large cities now use special vans to check on the air in different neighborhoods. These vans (like this one in New York City) are used to measure factory smoke and car fumes. If you belong to a Clean Air Club, ask if such a van can come and check the air in your neighborhood.

see, where, what time, and the date. If you have a camera, take a picture of any really bad pollution.

Is there a lot of soot where you live? You can take a soot sample as part of your detective work. You need half a dozen clean plastic cups, all the same size. Put a piece of cotton inside each cup. Then

If you are an active air-pollution detective, you may visit a modern factory like this one. In this New Jersey factory, the pollution-control systems get rid of most of the sulfur dioxide and also measure the smoke before it leaves the stack. The wiggly line on the paper in the engineer's hands shows part of one day's smoke measurement.

put the cups outdoors in out-of-the-way places such as roofs and ledges. Your cups should be near factories, schools, stores, gas stations, and apartment houses. Leave the cups for a week. When you collect the cups, number each one with a felt pen and keep a list of where each numbered cup spent the week. Arrange your cups from cleanest to dirtiest. What parts of your community have lots of soot? What parts have a little?

If you find a lot of air pollution in your community, ask your teacher or scout leader to display your records and pictures on a bulletin board. Also show your results to the mayor and other local officials. And your class should write letters to their congressmen and senators about it.

You could also try calling and writing to your local newspaper, radio, and TV stations. Ask for someone in charge of the news. Tell him what you have been doing. Perhaps you will be asked to make a report to your community.

If you want to do something about pollution outside your community, write to American business companies. If any member of your family owns stock in some companies, write to them, too. If not, get your local librarian to help you find a list of American companies and their main offices.

Compare your answers with other members of your Clean Air Club. If any of the letters you get from the companies do not seem clear, write again for more information.

Once you begin working to fight air pollution, you will find people of all ages who are interested in the same thing. And the more people do something about our polluted skies, the sooner *our dirty air* will become cleaner.

Will you grow up to look like this? Not if everyone does something about air pollution *now*.

Index

M

Mauro, Anthony, 15
Meuse Valley, Belgium, *33*
Mexico, 44
Montana, 18

N

Natural gas, 38, 42-43, 52-53
New York City, 9, 15, 25, 35, 38
New Zealand, 44
Nitrogen oxides, 16, 50, 51
Nixon, Richard, 51
North America, 11
Norway, 41, 52

O

Oil, 12, 41-42, 52-53
Oregon, 18
Oxygen, 12

P

Particles, definition of, 14
Pesticides, 21, 51
Philadelphia, Pennsylvania, 38
Philadelphia Zoo, 30
Photochemical pollution, 20
Pittsburgh, Pennsylvania, 45
Pollutants, definition of, 14. *See also* individual pollutants by name
Polluters, legal action against, 48-54, 55

Pollution. *See* Air pollution
Power plants, 16, 41, 50-51; hydro-electric, 44; steam, 44

S

Smog, 20, 28, 35
Smokestacks, 13, 16, 41, 50-51
South America, 11
Sprays, chemical, 21-24
Standards (air pollution), 51
State Pollution Control Board, 57
Sulfur dioxide, 41, 43
Sulfur oxides, 16, 30, 41-42, 51
Sunshine, effects of, 20, 25
Sweden, 41

T

Tokyo, Japan, 9-11, 31-32

U

Ueno Zoo, Tokyo, 30
United Nations, 52
United States, 9, 35, 41-44, 45-54

W

Washington, D.C., 9
Washington, state of, 18
Weather, effects of, 25-27, 33-35
Winds, effects of, 25-27, 28, 51
Windsor, Canada, 52